To live an *extraordinary life* is to pursue your purpose boldly, fulfil your dreams courageously, and touch the world with your presence.

Featured Writers

Meet our featured writers for *Extraordinary Life Magazine!*

Emily Gowor
Inspirational Writer, Author & Keynote Speaker
Founder of *Extraordinary Life*

Rieta Mistry
Feng Shui, Numerology, Colour & Flow Consultant

Dr Olivier Becherel
Personal Leadership Specialist, Life & Business Strategist

Michael Bromley
Martial Artist, Teacher & Mentor

Chanthy Ly
Holistic Wellness Coach, Therapist, Chef & Author

Mama Rae
Soul Food Cook & Universal Mum

Editorial

Dear readers,

Welcome to the launch issue of the *Extraordinary Life Magazine!*

This special publication was born out of my desire to share inspirational messages with humanity. See, I believe that every person is here on Earth with a purpose to fulfil and a gift to share with the world. I also believe that every human being deserves to thrive while fulfilling their calling in life.

My mission through the magazine is to empower, guide, inspire, and move you to do what you were born to do: to discover what you are here for, and live boldly in pursuit of that purpose. Our community of extraordinary speakers, coaches, mentors, leaders, healers, and authors will share from their heart and wisdom to help you live the most extraordinary life possible.

I invite you to savour each page, each article, and each section of the magazine. Take your time, reflect, and receive the information or message you need most at this stage of your journey. Allow it to inspire your mind, open your heart, and touch your soul.

You have unlimited, infinite potential and power at your core, and my goal is to support you to unlock that. Our ultimate vision is to see thousands more people living authentically, expressing what is within them, and making a significant impact on humanity.

Join us as we begin a heartfelt journey to leave a legacy on the planet.

Enjoy the launch issue!

With inspiration,

Inspirational Writer, Author & Keynote Speaker
Founder of *Extraordinary Life*

Contents

Issue 01

INSPIRATION & SPIRITUALITY

11. 7 Ways to Connect with Your Purpose

14. Nurturing Your Soul Connection

18. Life Lessons from the Chakras

21. The Power of Alternative Healing

22. Flow Tips for Your Life Path Number

ACHIEVEMENT & STRATEGY

31. 5 Steps to Live Your Life by Design

34. Overcome Your Financial Fears

38. Values: The Key to Achievement & Fulfilment

40. Your 4 Superpowers

WELLNESS & NOURISHMENT

49. Tapping into the Zen Way of Life

52. Ayurveda: A Pathway to Understand Your Body's Intelligence

54. Movement as a Gateway Within

58. Nourish Your Mind, Body, and Soul

60. Recipe: Turmeric Sweet Potato Wedges

RESOURCES

66. Journal Time

73. Your Reflections

76. Contact

Article Inquiries

Would you love to write for *Extraordinary Life Magazine*?

Do you have wisdom and inspiration that can make a difference in people's lives?

Would you love to share your personal story of overcoming adversity?

Apply to be a writer!

www.extraordinarylifemagazine.com

Inspiration & Spirituality

7 Ways to Connect with Your Purpose

These simple strategies will support you to connect with the deep meaning of your life

It is a natural human drive to wonder what our purpose in life is. We want to know who we are and why we are here on planet Earth. We know intuitively that being clear on and connected to our purpose is the core of a life we love. It is why we keep searching for it: the deeper meaning of our existence. We know intuitively that it is the key to an extraordinary future.

Although there are certainly people who discover their purpose in a sudden spiritual awakening – or who have known what they wanted to do since childhood – knowing our destiny doesn't always happen in a blinding flash of clarity.

Rather, like it does for many people, discovering your true purpose on the planet can occur as a series of moments. Moments where you 'get' who you are. Moments where you realise what you love to do. Moments where you catch a lasting glimpse of your destiny.

Although these moments may seem small at times, they are incredibly significant. They are the clues to the mystery, the pieces to the puzzle, the answer to who we truly are. It is in these moments that we discover what matters to us and can envision where it is that we want to go.

We see ourselves and our future clearly. These moments light the path ahead and show us how to navigate our human life on Earth.

The following are 7 ways to increase the frequency of these moments so that you can deepen your awareness of your divine purpose.

1. Spend quality time alone

How often do we take the time to connect inwardly? To connect with our heart and soul, who we truly are? Modern day life is busier than ever. We are continually surrounded by social media notifications, by people. We have responsibilities to fulfil and demands placed upon us daily.

In amongst the noise and chaos, it can be difficult to sit with your own heart and soul to discover what the deeper meaning of your life is. Unplugging from the noise of the world is a pathway to knowing your true self.

Start scheduling quality 'you' time into your diary. Make your relationship with yourself a top priority. Create the space for clarity to happen. Regular time alone can help you discover what you and your life are all about.

2. Cultivate deep gratitude

Are you deeply thankful for yourself? For the life you are living? For your past and your present? Or are you secretly wishing that it was different? When

you are in a grateful state, it not only clears your mind, but it opens your heart – and your purpose is a matter of the heart. It's something you feel, and when you feel it, you *know* it. This is why writing and verbalising your thankfulness is a powerful strategy to connect with your purpose.

Gratitude is a magnet for miracles and magic in your life – including discovering what you are here for – and the deeper the gratitude runs, the more blessings you will attract.

3. Learn to open your heart

Your heart is the centre of your power, and within it, lies the answer to your purpose in life. It is impossible to experience an open heart – to feel deep unconditional love – without receiving clarity about what matters in your life.

When you strip back the pain, what exists underneath it is only love and the truth of what you were born to do.

Going through life with a closed heart can close you off from your dreams. So, peel away the layers, open yourself up to the unconditional love within you, and get to the truth of what you care about most.

4. Inspire your senses

It's difficult to find your purpose if you sit inside all day staring at the wall. So, seek to inspire yourself through your senses: sight, sound, taste, and touch.

Listen to amazing music, get outside in nature, move your body, see great sights, surround yourself with beautiful things. Use the world around you to ignite the world within you. Allow your senses to awaken your soul.

5. Start journaling

Writing is a powerful pathway to develop your understanding of who you are. When you touch pen to page, you look and feel inwardly. You can ask yourself questions like *What inspires me? What am I interested in? What would I love to do with my life?* and receive the answers.

Taking even 10 minutes a day to reflect on your life, write down your thoughts, and explore your true feelings can fast-track your journey to knowing your purpose. Then you can spend less time wondering what it is, and more time fulfilling it.

6. Observe yourself

Each day, watch yourself from within. Notice what perks you up and what catches your attention. What are you naturally drawn to? What do you think about? What do you care about? What do you wish you could do? What do you dream about?

The answers are clues to your purpose. They are guiding you to your path of destiny and the extraordinary life you deserve. Your purpose is YOU. So, observe yourself over time. As you do, what truly matters to you and what inspires you deeply will become self-evident.

7. Communicate with God and your soul

Sometimes when I need clarity, I turn inward and upwards, and I ask God (life, the universe) for assistance. I surrender all my preconceived notions about who I am for a moment and give up my ego long enough to a) ask for help and b) receive it. I ask the divine to guide my life. And you know what? I've never prayed without receiving help.

———

Remember this as you move forwards on your journey: You are *meant to be here*. No, even more than that, you are *destined* to be here.

Your presence is needed. Your love is required. Your gifts are essential. Your message matters. Your actions count. Your mind is important. Your heart is everything. So, don't give up on finding your purpose. With patience, the light will shine through.

Emily Gowor is an Inspirational Writer, Author & Keynote Speaker devoted to helping people fulfil their purpose on Earth.

www.emilygowor.com

Extraordinary Life | 13

Nurturing Your Soul Connection

Brioni Faith shares why following soul aligned moments can lead to a meaningful life

You may have heard the expression, "Follow your bliss." When I first heard it, I thought it sounded a bit wishy-washy. It was a bit unrealistic and even a bit ungrounded. So, I didn't give it much importance. In fact, I was quite dismissive of it. I thought, 'Well, life can't always be like this. We all have to do things we don't like at some point.' That was, until the day I connected with its deeper meaning.

Have you ever found yourself thinking:

'If only my life could be fulfilling every day.'

'If only I knew what fulfilled me, and I could devote my life to it.'

The truth is, we are guided toward this every day. We only need to open ourselves to see it, hear it, and connect with it. To recognise it when it does present itself, and by doing so, nurture this connection. We all have key defining moments in our lives when we uncover something unique about ourselves.

These will be moments when you have surprised yourself, stretched yourself, and experienced a feeling of this energy coming *through* you, not from you. I call these **soul aligned** moments. So, how do we nurture this connection? How do we create more of these moments? This is where the line 'follow your bliss' began to make sense to me.

Think of your soul as your own personal source of light. It is the broadcaster, and our physical body is the receiver. Like a radio station, when we are tuned in, the signal strengthens, and we are able to receive more light and inspiration. Bliss is what you experience when your soul is aligned with your physical body. The higher centres of the brain are active, which allow insights and creativity to flow effortlessly. This is also called your "flow state."

Take a moment now to think about something you love doing, which brings you great joy. Think about the state you get into when you do this. Feel the energy, feel the flow. This is the feeling of your flow state.

Your flow state is the ultimate guide to your soul connection. It's where your greatest insights and inspiration occur. When you give yourself permission to follow this feeling, bathe in it, swim in it, explore it further, and follow your bliss, it will lead you to a greater understanding of who you are to be, and what you're here to share.

Your soul leaves clues, and it has been throughout your entire life.

Following your bliss, means following that which lights you up from the inside. When we are aligned to our flow state, we feel a sense of "stepping into the light" of who we truly are. When we align ourselves to the vibration of this flow state, our soul connection strengthens.

Nurturing your soul connection is about giving yourself complete permission to explore what brings you the greatest joy, bliss, and sense of deep fulfilment. Allowing yourself to shine your light from within, to honour your soul's expression, and to explore what you are here to share.

If you need more clarity on what brings you the greatest joy, perhaps make some time to journal on it. Explore those times in your life when you know you have felt the most inspired, the most creative and flowing. What were you doing? What was happening in those moments? How did it feel?

As we nurture our soul connection, we honour the light within ourselves. Our souls are always guiding us towards own unique expression, to help us achieve our fullest potential. Why? Because your light has come here to be seen, heard and shared.

Brioni Faith is a Transformational Healer & Musical Artist who helps people to reconnect with themselves, and bring about lasting change in their lives.

www.changeyourlife-academy.com/links

"You are being directed and redirected to fulfil your purpose 24 hours a day. Life is guiding you to your destiny."

EMILY GOWOR

Life Lessons from the Chakras

The wisdom of the energetic chakras can be a tool for growth and change

The chakras are a spinning vortex or wheel of light. They are the junctions that manage the flow of life force that runs through the energy body. Tuned into our life and life force energy, these energetic wheels of insight mirror back to us our current state, situation, or flow in life.

Depletions, excess, or blockages of these energy centres can manifest in our mental, emotional, and physical bodies and even affect our connection to the spirit world. Further than that, they hold much wisdom relating to life lessons that we all can benefit from.

When we are facing certain challenges in life, and we are feeling unmotivated or uninspired, chances are some of our chakras may be out of balance. Like a feedback system, specific chakras carry a myriad of information. For example, they can tell us areas where we may be pushing too hard in or why we are feeling stuck.

The chakras can help us reflect on the many personal aspects of our life. This is where the life lessons can come in and we can work to improve and grow in those areas, hence mastering those attributes. The seven main

chakra points and some examples of associated attributes with the relevant life lessons are as follows.

The **Base Chakra** can be associated with stability, security, and self-sufficiency. We can learn that taking responsibility for ourselves, our basic needs, self-care, and even financial stability, can lead to our physical wellbeing, as well as feeling grounded and secure in life.

The **Sacral Chakra** can be associated with our joy, creation, and sexuality. Here we can learn that looking after ourselves by allowing more joy into our lives, quite possibly through creative pursuits, can give a us a sense of feeling strong and open to change.

The **Solar Plexus Chakra** can be associated with self-confidence, self-worth, and personal power. In this area, we can learn about setting boundaries with our time and energy, as well as living an authentic life on our terms. This leads to feeling that we are in our power, self-confident with who we are, and worthy of pursuing our dreams.

The **Heart Chakra** can be associated with love. When we are able to love unconditionally, we can have empathy, understanding, and we can find it easier to forgive ourselves and others.

The **Throat Chakra** can be associated with communication, expression, and personal truth. The life lesson here is to speak your truth, and express and articulate yourself clearly and authentically.

The **Third Eye Chakra** can be associated with intuition, instincts, and a higher knowing. Life lessons here can be around trusting your gut, listening to your inner knowing, and trusting the feelings you experience, even on a vibrational level.

The **Crown Chakra** can be associated with divine, spirit connection, and a oneness with all. Life lessons here can be around our mental health as well as knowledge and spiritual enlightenment.

There are many resources available and ways in which you can work with the chakras. For example, through meditation, visualisation, breathwork, sound, vibration, and even intuition. A trained energy practitioner can give your chakra points a tune up and cleanse, as well as bring the energy back into balance.

By understanding the power of the chakras, you can raise your awareness of the potential impacts on different areas of your life and heal. Once we're tuned in, we can tune up our energy. We can reflect on and use these lessons from the chakras to master our life.

Alana Clare Power is an Inspirational Writer, Author, Yoga Teacher, and Pranic Healer on a quest to awaken, inspire, and live a soul-fuelled life.

www.alanaclarepower.com

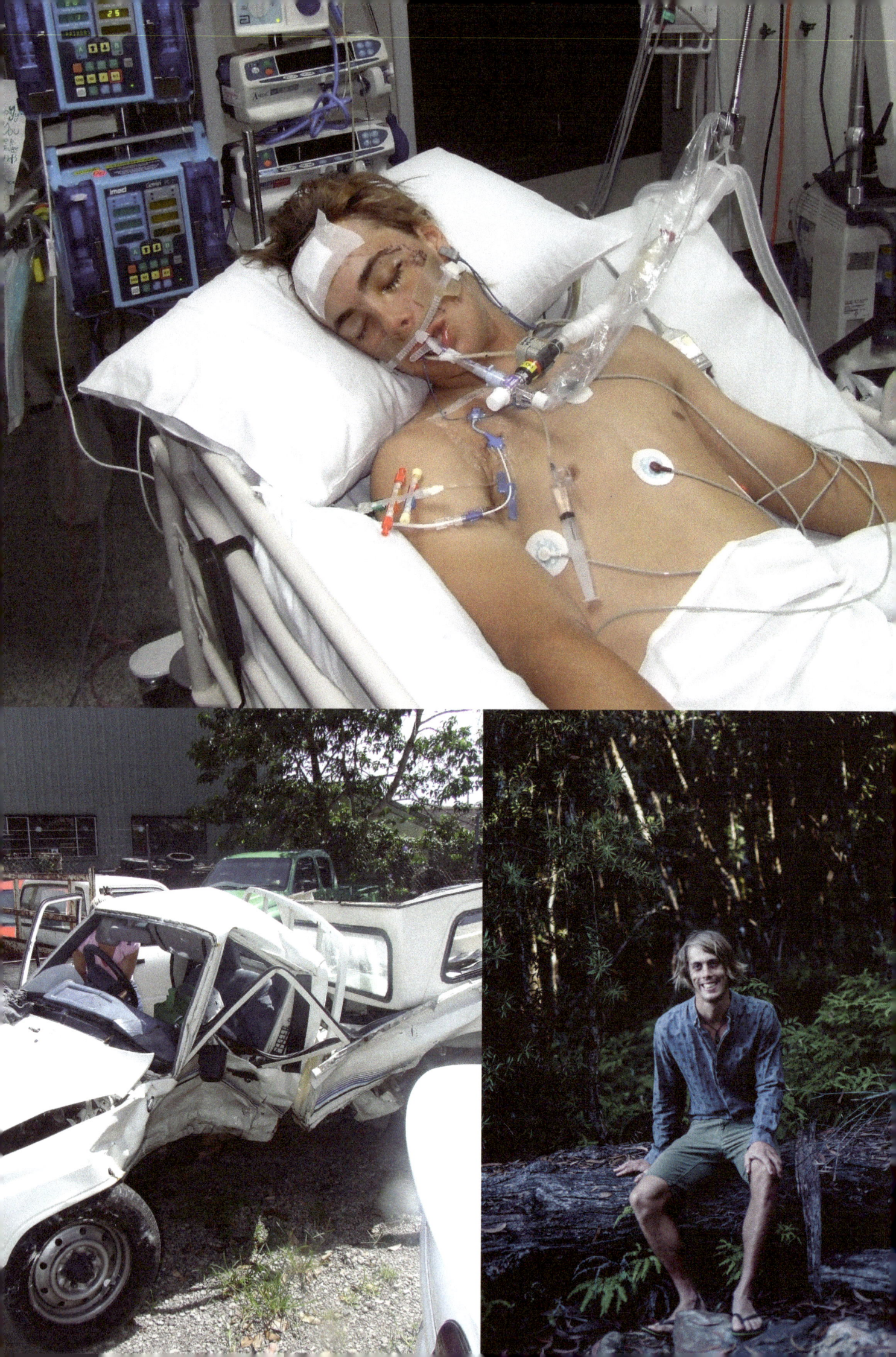

The Power of Alternative Healing

How Leroy overcame a car crash that nearly cost him his life

On November 22nd in 2007, I woke up at the usual time, 5:00 a.m. It was raining outside. After having breakfast and packing my lunch, I made a quick dash to my ute. I drove down the highway, barely able to see in front of me with the rain coming down hard.

As I exited the highway, my car began aquaplaning. I corrected the ute a few times before I decided to re-join the highway, but... I was too late. I collided with another car and my head hit the steering wheel.

The emergency services arrived and cut me out of the vehicle. I was rushed to the intensive care unit and put into an induced coma. I had a fracture to the pelvis, as well as bruises, and bleeding in my brain.

Seven days later, I woke up from the coma. I had many people around me, but no recollection of who they were. I was suffering from Post-Traumatic Amnesia. It took two weeks before I began to recognise my family and friends.

As I became stable, I started to do physiotherapy, occupational therapy, and speech pathology. I had to re-learn to walk and talk. The doctor told me I would never be able to do anything with my life.

I spent weekdays in the hospital and time with my family on the weekends. We spent our days at the beach, though my brain injury meant that I wasn't yet allowed to surf again. This was hard, as I loved to surf more than anything.

I became frustrated, as I wasn't allowed to do anything. I decided that this wasn't how I wanted to live my life. I began exploring self-help and alternative therapies including craniosacral therapy, chiropractic, and acupuncture.

Through persistence, I made a full recovery. I returned to work and got my license back within a year. Today, I am surfing again and living my dream as I help other people to find the healing they need in their mind and body. I live by my own limits, not what people say, and I am determined to leave my mark on this world.

Leroy Midgely is a Healer and Massage Therapist who shares his healing touch with people ready to restore their wellbeing from within.

www.earthhealingtouch.com

Flow Tips for Your Life Path Number

Apply these simple strategies to live with greater alignment and manifest the life you dream of

Everything has energy. This energy creates a vibration that either allows life to flow with effortless ease, or makes life seem like we are swimming against the tide.

The day you are born on is the first energy you are aligned to. It is the one vibrational moment that you have no control over and cannot change. This day plays a significant role in every moment of your life. It is your life path number.

This number gives you insight into your uniqueness: your strengths, talents, and the vibrational energies that allow your life to flow. This number is the core of who YOU are and can help to you discover your true self. To know your life path number, you must add:

Your birth day + your birth month + the year you were born.

Add them together, then reduce it to a single digit.

Example: 2 February 1967

02 + 02 + 1 + 9 + 6 + 7 = 27 (9)

This person's life path number is a 9.

Once you've calculated your number, here are some tips to help you start your journey back to your uniqueness.

Each life path number has a different vibration, and thus what will help you experience flow in your life will be different to what someone else born with another life path number may need.

1 Life Path: Colours like red and yellow support this path number. A clear view outside of your window is important.

2 Life Path: The colour to avoid here is black. Use orange and green. Images of two birds in the house can help the mind to feel like one is not alone.

3 Life Path: The colours turquoise and purple work well for this vibration. It's important that they see images of adventure and fun.

4 Life Path: It is important for this life path number to come from their heart, not from others' perceptions and expectations. The colour green gives the strength to come from self-love.

5 Life Path: Shades of blues and orange are fantastic for this path number. Cooking is a great way to stay in flow for this vibrational energy.

6 Life Path: Royal blue and indigo are both fabulous for the 6 life path. Responsibility is a key factor here. An image of the family gives strength.

7 Life Path: Purple, blues, and green are good. Solid colours are better than patterns and abstracts. Trees are very important to help you feel grounded.

8 Life Path: Florals and patterns in the colours of pink and cream. It is important to be surrounded by images of abundance. Pictures of arid land or empty objects create an unsettling energy within the body.

9 Life Path: White and purple work well for this path number. Ensure that there are no unfinished projects lying around the house as this will slow your flow down.

Allow these few tips to help you go back home to your core: your unique blueprint. Remember that in every moment you are being influenced by what you expose yourself to.

What are your eyes seeing every day? What is the message being translated by your brain? What are you manifesting in your life in any given moment?

I look forward to hearing from you about the changes that you have experienced by connecting to your uniqueness.

Rieta Mistry is a Flow Consultant who uses the power of colour, numerology, and Feng Shui to support people in manifesting the life they dream of.

www.rietamistry.com

Quick Takeaways

1

You have an important purpose to fulfil on Earth. It is buried within your heart and soul. Your purpose is waiting to be discovered.

2

Your 'Flow State' is the ultimate guide to your soul connection. It is where your greatest insights and inspiration occur.

3

Your Chakras can provide a powerful access to the lessons you most need to learn in life. You can use these 7 energy centres as a pathway to spiritual empowerment.

Quick Takeaways

4

No matter what you face, deep healing is possible. You can overcome even the most adverse circumstances and fulfil your purpose.

5

Understanding your Life Path number can help you tap into greater flow and manifest the life you desire.

6

You deserve to thrive on all levels and in all areas of your life. The extraordinary future you dream of is possible.

REFLECTIONS ON PURPOSE

This book shares 30 inspirational writings on how to find and fulfil your soul's calling

FREE FENG SHUI CONSULTATION!

Explore the obstacles in your environment that are holding you back from manifesting your dreams

Saramatu

BREAK FREE AND CONNECT WITH YOURSELF!

Download this free e-book to become aware of the human programs running your life and how to break them

Earth Healing Touch

Through touch, we create flow.
Through connection, we create change.

UNWIND YOUR MIND, BODY & SOUL!

Receive $20 off your first healing massage with Leroy Midgley

Achievement & Strategy

5 Steps to Live Your Life by Design

Dr Olivier Becherel reveals the keys to create a life and career you love from within

Gallups's State of the Global Workplace report showed that a growing number of people feel trapped in a miserable job, where the only thing getting them out of bed in the morning is the apparent security of their paycheque.

Instead of living by design, many people are staying safe and playing a smaller game than the one they are capable of. However, it doesn't have to be this way. Instead of letting life happen to you, you can be the creator of your future. The key to this is personal leadership.

What is **personal leadership?**

Personal leadership is the ability to utilise your innate leadership traits and natural qualities to guide the direction of your life and career, instead of letting time, chance, and external circumstances to determine your course.

Developing personal leadership allows you to know in your heart that you are on the right path, because you have a clear sense of direction that comes from within.

You have a compelling vision to move towards, you are connected to your purpose, and you express your unique talents to make an impact in a rewarding and meaningful career of your choice.

In a nutshell, you experience more satisfaction, inspiration, and vitality, because you intentionally shape your destiny with every decision you make and every action you take.

How do you do that? Below are 5 steps that will help you activate your *personal leadership* and create a clear path forward to bring more meaning, income, and fulfilment in your life, by doing what you love, making a difference, and building a legacy.

Step 1: Clarify Your Identity

Being clear on who you are and fully understanding your values, thought patterns, decisions, actions, and behaviours, is crucial. It allows you shift into the driver's seat of your life. From there, you can find and grow a career and life that will optimise your strengths and gifts, and fulfil you.

By knowing who you are and what you value, you can make important decisions to allocate and manage your most precious resources: *time*, *space*, *energy*, *money*, and *relationships*. It unlocks the compass to follow your path of least resistance, personally and professionally.

Step 2: Claim Your Inner Wealth

Owning your talents, uniqueness, and worth, is vital in life. Deep inside, many of us experience an insidious feeling that can derail our mental and emotional strength and limit our opportunities in life. I'm sure you're familiar with 'impostor syndrome'.

When the impostor syndrome creeps in, you feel not good enough or not worthy. You then feel the need to 'prove your worth', which can often lead to unsustainable and draining behaviours to overcompensate.

In the long run, this can seriously impact your health, life, and career, making it feel like you're constantly running on a treadmill and living in the rat race.

Breaking through the impostor syndrome and letting your own true magnificence shine forth confidently will happen when you claim your inner wealth. This means acknowledging and owning your talents, genius, and unique competitive advantage.

Once you've established the value you offer to the world, you will feel comfortable to declare your worth and express yourself in the form of a service to those around you.

Step 3: Clear the Roadblocks

Life is a journey in which we all encounter temporary obstacles and setbacks. While we may encounter physical obstacles, mental and emotional blocks (such as limiting beliefs or negative emotions) are the most confronting, and often hold us back from playing a bigger game in life.

The ability to decode the messages and lessons contained within those

roadblocks is what sets apart inspired and successful individuals from the rest. Instead of blaming the world, other people, or their circumstances, for their 'misfortune', they focus on discovering how they can harness the wisdom contained within these experiences to make quantum jumps in awareness, confidence, and resilience.

Instead of shying away from challenges, embrace them fully. Use them as steppingstones towards unlocking your greatness. This essential skill will bring your vision and mission alive and catapult your life to new heights.

Step 4: Create Your Future Vision

Every act of creation starts with an intention, a reason, and a vision. These provide the foundation to a clear path forward and help guide you in decision-making and execution. Without a clear and compelling destination to move towards, the status-quo will persist.

Without connecting with your future vision and purpose in life, you will be destined to follow someone else's vision, with the possibility that it may lead somewhere you don't really want to be.

That is why if you truly desire to live by design, then it's your responsibility to identify your 'why', your vision, your mission, and your purpose. You can do this by looking at the bigger picture of your life. Furthermore, besides helping you stay on track, creating your future vision will also provide with you much needed inspiration in tough times.

Step 5. Commit to Yourself

Every individual has a particular way of doing things. This is a natural flow based on their unique energetic blueprint that gives them the ability to design, and implement, authentic strategies to get the results they are aiming for.

When you commit to yourself, you can achieve optimum performance and live by design in your own terms, not by default.

When you live according to your own design and follow your authentic strategies, the right opportunities will show up to help you grow and accelerate both your personal and professional success.

_____

Applying these 5 steps will support you to activate your personal leadership, share your gift with the world, and create the life and career you love.

Dr. Olivier J. Becherel, PhD, is a Personal Leadership Specialist, Life & Business Strategist who helps high-achieving professionals to break through to the next level of their life and career.

www.drolivierbecherel.com

Overcome Your Financial Fears

Financial fitness coach Jo Outram shares simple advice to transform your relationship with money and create wealth

You desire more wealth, but you avoid the truth about your financial situation. You want to be richer, but you don't manage your money on a regular basis. You feel that you deserve more financial abundance, but you hold back from talking about it to your nearest and dearest. Sound familiar?

You are not alone if you think about and behave towards money in this way. Most people experience fear when it comes to addressing their money matters. While the primary role of fear is to keep you safe, when it comes to money, it often becomes restrictive and even paralysing. It stops us from doing what we need to do to expand our wealth.

By implementing these three simple strategies, you can start to overcome your fears, create a new relationship with money, and achieve financial mastery.

1. Start with small action steps

The do-nothing strategy is straight out of the fear playbook. Unfortunately, it is one of the riskiest money strategies. While doing nothing might make you feel safe temporarily, you aren't protected or secure financially. Imagine building your home on the top of a mud hill. You feel safe. But what if there was torrential rain or a severe drought? Suddenly the foundations you believed were safe no longer support you.

Start to take simple action on your finances to build solid foundations.

- **Set a weekly 'money date'**

Use this time to file your paperwork or pay your bills. Start by decluttering your financial paperwork, and then keep it up to date with a simple filing system.

- **Set financial goals**

This might involve paying off a portion of your debt in the next six months or saving a set amount in the next 90 days.

2. Beat procrastination

Every time you avoid taking care of your finances, you are unconsciously sending a message to yourself that, "I am not worth the effort." There are, however, things that you can start to do to stop this cycle.

How much money do you allocate in the areas of housing, debt repayment, food, savings, and discretionary spending, Are you up to date with your debt repayments? Have you reviewed your retirement plans recently? Is your income stable? Can you generate more?

When you have the list of your answers, break each area down into bite-sized steps. Then on each 'money date', simply select an item and act on it.

3. Get comfortable talking about money

Avoiding money talk is a bias that is tightly woven into our culture. We don't talk about how much we earn, how much we save, or how much debt we have. We also don't talk about how we feel about wealth. It appears that everything relating to money is off limits.

Often, it's because we feel ashamed about not understanding financial matters. Understanding the basics of money management is key to facing this fear. Implement the suggestions above to get you started. Then, when you feel brave enough, why not start a conversation about money with someone close to you? Ask a question or source advice.

_____

Understanding and admitting to the fear you feel around money is the first step to transforming your financial situation. By becoming aware of how it influences your feelings around wealth, you can start to overcome the barriers that are stopping you from mastering your finances.

Jo Outram is a Financial Educator, Author & Mindset Coach dedicated to helping people eliminate the blocks to financial success.

www.jooutram.com

"To say that you have much to share with the world is a great understatement.
Your value is infinite."

EMILY GOWOR

Values: The Key to Achievement & Fulfilment

Human behaviour expert Dr John Demartini reveals why knowing your highest values can help you to master your life

I have been researching and teaching personal development and human behavior since 1972. Out of all the principles and methodologies I have been blessed to explore and study, human values is one of the most significant.

See, every human being (consciously or unconsciously) lives by a set of priorities, a set of values. This is what they consider to be the most important to the least important activities in their life. Stop and think about that for a minute. How you perceive the world, what you decide to do, and how you act, is all based on your hierarchy of values.

Therefore, knowing what is highest on your unique list of values, and learning how to live by your highest priority can completely transform your life.

Your highest value is where you tend to be the most inspired and where you feel the most fulfilled. It may be perceived as being your heartfelt 'why' or your meaningful mission. It is the key to your purpose in life. It is where you tend to be the most objective, balanced, resilient, adaptable, disciplined, reliable, and focused.

Your highest value is what you are most likely to build momentum toward and excel at. When you set a goal that is aligned with this value, you become spontaneously inspired to act on it. This means that you have the highest probability of achieving that outcome. You are also more likely to embrace whatever challenges you may face in the pursuit of the goal. It is the individuals who live according to their highest value who tend to rise up in leadership, produce original work, and leave a lasting legacy in the world.

Answering these 13 questions from my Value Determination Process will assist you to discover your authentic hierarchy of values. Your life demonstrates what matters to you. Identify the top three answers to each question.

1. What do you fill your primary personal or professional space with most?

2. How do you primarily spend your time when you are awake?

3. How do you spend your energy? What energises you most?

4. What do you spend your money on most?

5. Where are you most organised and ordered?

6. Where are you most reliable, disciplined, and focused?

7. What do you inwardly think about most?

8. What do you visualise, and then realise, most?

9. What do you internally dialogue with yourself about most?

10. What do you talk about most to others in social settings?

11. What inspires you most? What is common to those individuals, insights, experiences, or events that inspire you most?

12. What are your most consistent long-term goals that you are pursuing that are showing evidence of coming true?

13. What do you love learning, reading, studying, or listening about the most?

Reflect on your life now and answer what it is, instead of what you think SHOULD be a priority. The repeated answers that are written the most frequently, second most frequently and third most frequently will be your top three highest values.

For example, your life may demonstrate that your career, business, health, or your family is your highest value. Regardless of what it is, give yourself permission to discover what is truly important to you.

Your hierarchy of values dictates your destiny. So, give yourself permission to be you. The magnificence of who you are is far greater than any fantasy you may impose on yourself.

Dr John Demartini is a world-renowned human behavior expert, internationally published author, a global educator, and the founder of the Demartini Method, a revolutionary tool in modern psychology.

www.drdemartini.com

Extraordinary Life | 39

Your 4 Superpowers

Use the unique power of your mind to create change and live your best life

Most of us are unaware of the four incredible superpowers we possess. But these **four superpowers** are available to everyone. They are the nuts and bolts of how to get into the driver's seat to create the life of your dreams.

1. Perception

Your first superpower is the ability you have to change your life by *altering your perception*. **Your sense of reality is determined by your own perspective.** Both your upbringing and experiences literally program you with your individual perception, creating your own version of reality, until you see from a broader perspective. You get what you focus on, and **you** get to *decide* what that is – it's *your* choice! Activating Superpower #1 requires you to open your mind by asking yourself:

- What have I not noticed here?
- How could I look at this situation or event differently?

Expanding your perception brings greater clarity.

2. Clarity

If you're not clear about who you are, what you want, or why you want it, challenges may distract or discourage you, and throw you off-course. Your identity revolves around what matters most to you. Whatever you value most, your top priority, ultimately determines your identity and your path through life. The true you is expressed through your highest priorities.

To activate Superpower #2, get clear on what matters most to you. When you have clarity, you can live more easily on priority.

3. Priority

Prioritising what matters most to you creates opportunities, allows ideas to come, and guides you in the direction you want to go. Developing the habit of daily planning and reviewing to set realistic and flexible goals which are aligned with your top priorities is the best way to activate Superpower #3.

4. Feedback

We each have an incredible in-built mechanism providing vital feedback: Superpower #4. Whether or not you realise it, everything that happens in your life is designed to wake you up to who you truly are, so you can honour yourself and live your best life. The innate intelligence running through you is your personal homeostatic feedback mechanism, like a GPS, constantly providing updates designed to help you stay aligned with your top priorities. The further you stray from what matters most or who you truly are, the more feedback you will receive. This can manifest itself in physical, emotional, or mental challenges.

Once you become aware and expand your perception, you will notice the feedback, and create the habit of *responding* rather than *reacting*.

Activate Superpower #4 by listening to the feedback life gives you. Pay attention to the whispers of your feelings before they turn into screams of pain or trauma. Developing this reflective awareness is a habit created over time. Asking this question is a great place to start:

- How is this situation or issue benefiting me and helping me to achieve what matters most?

This 'formula for success' isn't the quick-fix way, but using these superpowers daily allows true transformation leading to a fulfilling, meaningful life.

Sally Lewis is an Author, Educator & Mentor on a mission to equip students of all ages with the tools required to navigate the challenges of an increasingly uncertain future.

www.sallylewis.com

Quick Takeaways

1

Discovering your innate qualities, strengths, and values will empower you to build a career that fulfils you.

2

Small action steps, together with a commitment to yourself, will help you to overcome your financial fears and create wealth.

3

Every person has unique value to offer the world. This emerges from their values.

Quick Takeaways

4

Knowing and living congruently with your highest values is the key to a life of accomplishment, meaning, and impact.

5

Use your perception, inner clarity, priorities, and the feedback within and around you to unlock your power.

6

Personal leadership means knowing, respecting, loving, and being yourself in the world.

Dr Olivier Becherel
Activate Your Personal Leadership

YOUR FREE CLARITY SESSION!

Identify your authentic path forward to level up in your life, career or business

Sally Lewis

FIGURE OUT YOUR FUTURE

Order a signed copy of the book with limited edition bookmark for just $29.99!

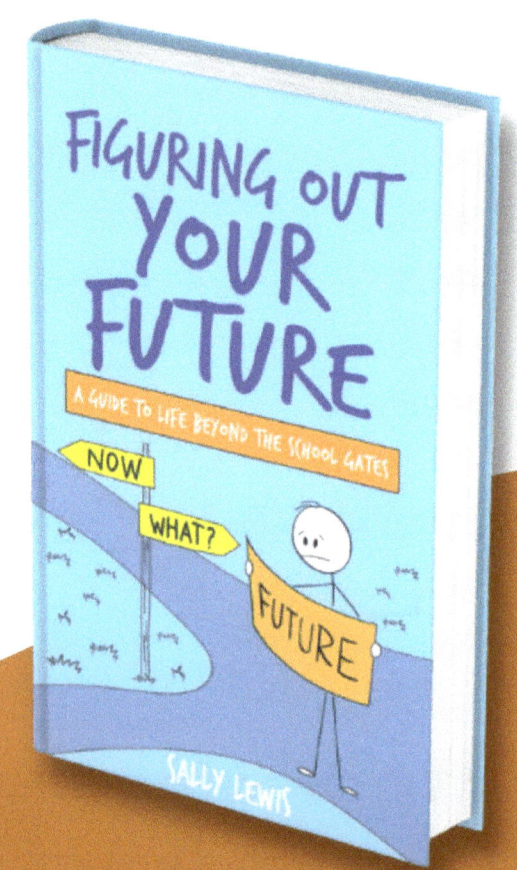

DISCOVER YOUR MONEY PERSONALITY PROFILE

This free profile will reveal your natural money gifts and challenges, so you can generate wealth with ease!

FREE DREAM LIFE PLANNER!

Design the future that inspires you with the dream life planner template

Wellness & Nourishment

Tapping into the Zen Way of Life

Discover 5 ancient universal principles to help you find your inner balance and experience flow in any situation

Life can be overwhelming at times. There's no avoiding the stressful situations or emotional trials that come up, but there are **five universal life principles** that can help you navigate these with ease and flow. These can be mapped across to the fundamental areas of being human.

There are many principles, which are the basis of universal laws, doctrines, philosophies and truths. However, these **five principles** were broad enough to help me recognise and develop a clear pathway to my Dharma and purpose. Once I acquired this knowledge, my universe unfolded like a divine wave. I sincerely trust that these principles will guide, serve, and assist you as well.

For personal development, it seems essential to categorise and understand the areas of life. Most human behavioural experts embrace seven or eight *areas*.

If we strip back things like career, money, relationships, community and so on, what remains is the **Physical, Mental, Emotional,** and **Spiritual** areas. These are the four realms we can apply these five universal principles to.

1: Agility

How mobile are you in your body? Are you agile? The meaning of this principle is being able to change direction with ease and grace.

However, **agility** is not only an important principle in fitness, but also for the human pathway. Regarding the emotions that we feel – negative emotions, in particular – the agility principle reminds us to consider how long we want to feel this way. Can we change to a more constructive mood? Can we alter what we feel and balance ourselves more swiftly?

We can adjust and get on with the new or altered task without clinging to the emotion that no longer serves us. If stress is the inability to adapt to changing circumstances, then having an agile mind will certainly aid in escalating you to a heightened level of emotional intelligence.

2: Balance

Balance is an amazing principle that resonates with all of life, universal laws, and the way of nature itself! Everything in existence must have its opposite. The opposing energies and forces must balance for there to be synergy and harmony, like Yin and Yang.

We can use the **balance** principle to maintain a position of relative stability. *Still* the mind and create space for self-awareness. A principle-based solution is to look for the middle way: the path that works for you. Balance can also represent the important oscillation between work (effort) and taking time out to rejuvenate and recharge.

3: Clarity

Clarity is all about your life purpose, direction, fulfillment, and your inner truth put into practice. In the spiritual realm, clarity is having the ability to light your own pathway in cloudy situations.

Have you ever felt the type of inspiration that washes over you like looking at a cloudless blue sky? Or standing under a shower of water? What occurs here? It is the present moment where the wisdom of the elements and the universe are speaking to you! This is clarity.

You can ask yourself quality questions to increase your clarity. Is the pathway to my goals and outcomes clear? How can I deal with obstacles and procrastination? What strategy action can I take that will dissolve confusion and mystery? What am I truly trying to achieve? How do I want to spend my time, energy, and space?

A pathway to clarity is to set an intention or a goal that has *value* to *you*! Clarity on your values will reveal your *vision* for the future and your mission in life.

4: Flexibility

Being inflexible can limit your ability to live in alignment with your authentic self. Rigidity can also limit you from discovering your real purpose. Maybe it's time to break the mould and be *flexible*.

If you are being asked to bend outside of the normal rules or boundaries that you are accustomed to, flexibility supports a willingness to compromise. Flexibility is about being adaptable,

limber, and pliant. It is to bend easily without breaking.

Embodying the flexibility principle does not mean that you will sacrifice what is important to you. Instead, it gives you greater strength, because you can flow with life's circumstances and obstacles instead of becoming so rigid that you break.

Where are you holding on too tightly to something that does not work anymore? What other options or pathways are there to live the future you desire? Where can you let go, give it love, and flow to achieve your outcomes? What degrading feelings can you release?

5: Strength

What is the meaning of *strength*? What does it mean for you? It is the quality of being strong and having the capacity for reliance, exertion, or endurance. This sounds like a quality that we'd all like to have, right? Perhaps we could incorporate strength as one of our life principles.

Strength of mind means having courage, resilience, willpower and determination. It is endeavouring to always *do* or *be* better. A by-product of strength is gentleness. It is said that if you don't have strength of mind and body, you have no control over your actions.

Using these five principles can spark and guide your personal evolution. I would now like to encourage you to think of a situation you are currently facing.

Next, identify how the situation relates to the *four realms* and which of the principles can support you best. For example, you might be having difficulty in your job or career.

"If I was more *agile* or *flexible* of *mind* and *emotion*, I could respond or act more appropriately." (*Emotional intelligence*)

"Perhaps I just need to have *strength* of *mind* to push through today!" (*Willpower*)

Having clear communications with your colleagues or manager may ease the issue. Alternatively, *clarity* on an exit strategy may *balance* your life and make it more purposeful and fulfilling.

Our highest priority, perhaps, is to radiate and integrate these principles so we can become our most powerful, abundant, and unlimited self.

Michael Bromley is a Martial Artist, Teacher, Trainer and Mentor devoted to guiding people on their path of personal evolution.

Ayurveda: A Pathway to Understand Your Body's Intelligence

How honouring your unique body type and balancing your doshas creates lasting wellness

Ayurveda is the science of life, lifespan, and longevity. *AYU* means **life** and *VEDA* means **science**. Ayurveda is the world's most ancient, scientific, holistic, complete, and natural system of health care which has been around for over 5000 years.

The seat of Ayurveda is in the doshas. The word **dosha** means *energy*. The doshas consist of the five elements we experience around us: earth, water, fire, air, and ether (space). These elements come together from birth to create the three doshas, which are also known as mind-body types. They are unique blends of physical, emotional, and mental characteristics.

These natural elements are reflected in our bodies. *Fire* is hot and powerful, like the digestive system. It consists of light, heat, transformation, and metabolism. *Water* is fluid and cool, like our lymphatic system, flow, and liquidity. *Earth* is dense and grounding, like our structure, solidity, and stability. *Air* is light and moving, like our breath, motion, and nourishment. *Ether* is the vastness that exists inside us when we still our minds, space, and container.

No one has a body that is entirely one dosha, but rather we are a combination of all three: Vata, Pitta and Kapha. Ayurveda is a system of regaining our innate balance, so we always treat the dosha that is out of balance in the body.

Vata is *Air + Ether*. It's associated with bodily movements like breathing, muscle contraction, and heart function. Someone who is Vata dominant might be thin, feel cold often, and have dry skin.

An imbalance in the Vata dosha can result in anxiety, fear, and digestive issues like constipation. This can cause difficulty falling asleep and occasionally anxiety. If this sounds like you as a Vata, work on increasing your Pitta (fire) warming, stimulating, and Kapha (Earth) grounding energies to regain balance.

Pitta is *Fire + Water*. The Pitta dosha is thought to control the endocrine, metabolic, and digestive systems. People who are predominantly Pitta can have a medium build and have acne-prone skin. They tend to be busy, high-achieving, and dominant individuals.

An imbalance in Pitta can also lead to anger, overexertion, and burnout, as well as skin irritation (including chronic acne), rashes, and acidity. Excess Pitta (heat) in the body causes issues like heartburn, hyperacidity, and even ulcers. You will need to work on increasing your Vata (wind) and Kapha (Earth) energies to regain balance.

Kapha is *Earth + Water*. Kapha is a stabilising energy thought to supply water to the body and maintain the immune system. Someone who is Kapha dominant is calm, grounded, and forgiving. Imbalance in Kapha can lead to jealousy, sluggishness, and weight gain.

By having excess Kapha in the body, you will feel low in energy. It can be hard to get up in the morning and get the body moving. You may gain weight and retain water easily, especially if you eat sweets, carbohydrates, and dairy. You may also have a sluggish digestive system, a slower metabolism, and some mucus build up (such as nasal congestion, sore throat, coughs, colds, or infections).

Kapha are always taking care of others and may neglect self-care since they put the needs of others first. If this sounds like you, work on increasing Vata (Air) and Pitta (fire) energy to regain balance.

Ayurveda encourages certain lifestyle interventions and natural therapies to regain a balance between the body, mind, spirit, and the environment. Ayurveda can have a positive effects and health benefits when used as a complementary therapy in combination with standard, conventional medical care.

Chanthy Thong is a Holistic Health Wellness Coach, Therapist, Chef & Author who is passionate about helping and transforming people health around the world to live and create an extraordinary life.

www.chanthyintowellness.com

Extraordinary Life | 53

Movement as a Gateway Within

Yoga instructor Kim McGrath shares 3 simple ways to bring movement back into your life and reconnect to yourself daily

The importance of physical activity and the need to move has been ingrained in our minds and bodies since we were running around joyously with muddy faces as a kid. Back then, moving just happened. We were tuned into our internal energy and its need to be released.

As we move through life, our movement becomes a way to connect to others and ourselves. Then somehow, overtime, that intuition to move begins to dim as life becomes busy and we start families and build our careers. We become time poor, opening the door to overwhelm and stress. The space and time required for regular movement becomes an unwelcome guest.

Life-changing events are usually the catalyst for change. Those moments throw light back on the importance to reconnect and move again. This call-to-action floodlights the need to make changes and accept that movement is an integral part of fulfilling on-going, positive long-term health. So, how can we intertwine natural physical movement back into our busy lives?

Over the past ten years, I have explored and adapted ways that movement could intentionally be integrated into the day. As a working mother, time is constantly a precious commodity and accepting the importance of keeping my physical body and mind functioning well has brought a sense of steadiness, self-worth, and joy. I have discovered three simple ways, all of which are sustainable, time-friendly, and allow one to reconnect within:

1. Habit-Stacking

Habit stacking is both a simple and accessible way to integrate movement into your day. By pairing up your desired movement with a habit that you already perform, you create an intention that already slots into your daily flow.

For example, when brush your teeth in the morning, do 5 lunges. Brushing your teeth is the current habit and already ingrained into your routine. This action will then trigger the new movement habit: 5 lunges.

2. Find a Buddy

Buddying up is a great technique, as having another person to keep you accountable is a powerful motive. Our natural instinct is to not let our buddy down and we are more likely to drag ourselves out of bed on that cold, frosty morning to go for a walk when we know our friend is waiting for us. This technique not only motivates us to move, but also gifts us with someone else's time, and allows us to come together with a purpose – plus it is fun!

3. Make It Simple

Simple feels good! The simpler the task, the more you will want to do it. It's also just as important to make your intention to move visible, not only to yourself, but to those around you.

This visibility – whether that is setting up your yoga space or laying out your walking shoes – cements your intention of the movement behaviour you are creating. It also shows those around you that your wellbeing is a priority and makes you more accountable for your actions.

Bringing simple movement into your day does NOT have to be a hard slog. Allow yourself to explore and discover all kinds of movement, whether you are dancing in your living room, walking with your friend, or moving on your yoga mat. Allow your movement to be the fuel that moves you with a sense of stability and connection through your day.

Not only will your physical body sing to your new movement habits, but your mind and soul will find a sense of self-worth, motivation, and purpose, that will plant a seed of steadiness within you. This is one of the greater gifts of movement.

Kim McGrath is a yoga therapist, a mum, and a writer who is devoted to inspiring people to move, reconnect, and be the best versions of themselves through regular self-care and simple and sustainable practices.

www.kindredyoga.com.au

"Your body is your only point of contact with planet Earth. So, love it."

EMILY GOWOR

Nourish Your Mind, Body and Soul

The growing importance of eating healthy nutritious food in a stressed modern world

For most of my life, I have been interested in food and health, researching and learning as much as I could from different sources. Both my mother and father passed away from cancer, and although I was determined not to suffer the same fate, my journey didn't actively start until I was listening to an interview on the radio in the 1970's.

Vicki the Vego was being interviewed, and of the half hour interview, I only recall one thing she said. It was that three days after a lemon is picked from the tree, there is no Vitamin C left in the lemon!

This makes sense considering that vitamin C is a water-soluble vitamin, and so it evaporates through the skin of fruit and vegetables.

I was blessed to have grown up on a farm where we had fresh meat, grew some of our vegetables, and had orchards nearby. My mum cooked everything from scratch without using additives.

When I married and lived on four acres of land near Eildon in Victoria, we grew as much as we could. It was in those months when we were eating the food we grew, that we felt the most alive and vital.

But the way we eat, and what we eat, has radically changed in the past fifty years, and that impacts our health. This is shown by the latest health report conducted by the Australian Institute of Health & Welfare (AIHW):

- 47% (11.6 million) of Australians have one or more chronic health conditions
- Two in three Australian adults are overweight or obese
- Three in ten adults do not get enough physical exercise
- Fewer than one in ten adults eat greens each day, and 96% of men and 87% of women do not eat the recommended amount of vegetables per day
- One Australian is diagnosed with diabetes every 8 minutes

Unfortunately, this trend is happening around the world, not just here in Australia. While life expectancy rates are continuing to rise, almost half of humanity are living with at least one chronic health condition.

It is estimated that one in five deaths globally is linked with poor diet, as well as contributing to various chronic diseases.

People are now consuming high amounts of trans fats, sugary drinks, processed foods, and a large amount of red meat instead of healthy foods like fruit, vegetables, nuts, seeds, and whole grains.

What does this mean in terms of our health and wellbeing? For us to get back to having optimal health, we need to look what we are putting into our bodies daily. Ask yourself these questions:

How nourishing is your food?

Are you eating a balanced diet?

Are you present when you cook your food?

Are you present when you eat your food?

Are you sitting down when you eat?

Are you continuing to work while you eat?

Are you eating more takeaways?

Are you grateful for everything and everyone who took part in getting the food to your plate?

Food is information for our body. The better the quality of the food is, the better quality of the information that our body gets – and the better you will feel in your mind, body, and soul.

Mama Rae is an extraordinary cook and universal mum whose mission is to bring love and joy into people's lives.

www.mamarae.com.au

Extraordinary Life | 59

Turmeric Sweet Potato Wedges

Gluten Free, Dairy Free & Vegan

This is one of my absolute favourite side dishes. It tastes yummy alongside many other meals, from vegetable curries to barley loaf and roasts.

They are always a big hit with friends and family. Making them is as easy as falling off a log!

Shopping List

- 2 large sweet potatoes
- 2 tablespoons chickpea flour (Besan flour)
- 1 tablespoon turmeric
- 3 tablespoons coconut oil
- Salt
- Black pepper

The How-To Part

1. Preheat oven to 200 degrees Celsius
2. Grease a baking tray or line it with baking paper
3. Melt the coconut oil in a pot on the stove on low heat
4. Add the chickpea flour and turmeric to the coconut oil
5. Stir through so that it is mixed well
6. Add more oil (a tablespoon at a time) if the paste is too thick
7. Cut the potatoes into wedges and place on prepared tray
8. Pour the turmeric mixture over the wedges
9. Stir the wedges to coat with the turmeric mix
10. Roast for 40 minutes or until cooked (soft)
11. Enjoy!

Secrets From Mama Rae's Kitchen

- You can prepare white potato wedges the same way. However, sweet potato has more nutritional value and is a lower GI food, so it is more nourishing.
- I love turmeric. I usually add double the amount (just add a little extra oil to keep the paste consistency).
- You could use other flour besides chickpea. If you do, just be aware that the flavour of the wedges will be quite different.

Wellness Tip

The reason we add black pepper to the mixture is because black pepper activates curcumin – the active ingredient in turmeric. This makes the recipe anti-inflammatory.

Quick Takeaways

1

Apply the principles of agility, balance, clarity, flexibility, and strength to overcome challenges and navigate your way forwards.

2

Ayurveda provides us with an understanding of our unique physical body and what it needs for us to thrive.

3

By tuning in to the innate wisdom within our mind, heart, soul, and body, we can master our lives.

Quick Takeaways

4

By bringing simple physical movement back into our daily life - and making it fun - we can experience a greater level of wellbeing and wholeness.

5

In today's world, it is more important than ever for us to nourish ourselves with quality food, fluids, and habits.

6

Preparing nutritious and delicious meals can be easy when you know how. Simplicity is the key.

FREE 18 MINUTE YOGA SESSION

Enjoy a time-friendly flowing yoga session designed to move & reconnect the whole body!

 SCAN ME

JOIN MAMA RAE'S SOUL FOOD EKITCHEN

Learn to cook nutritious delicious gluten & dairy free food online!

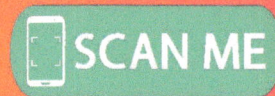 SCAN ME

ZEN MOVEMENT
FOR LIFE

SCAN ME

MASTER THE ART OF ZEN YOGA!

Learn gentle daily movement that will increase your vitality & wellness

EXTRAORDINARY Life

ORDER THE PRINTED MAGAZINE!

Take this magazine wherever you go for the inspiration and guidance you need

SCAN ME

Journal Time

It's journal time!

Journalling provides us with the space to pour our feelings onto the page.

It brings us back to our truth and allows us to access the answers we need.

This alone makes it a profound practice to work with daily – and a reliable source of creativity and inspiration.

There is no judgement when you journal.

It's a record just for you – and it's there 24 hours a day. It is a sacred and safe space for you to be yourself, express what is within you, and find your way to the other side of whatever you are facing in your life today.

Use the following questions and pages to reflect inwardly on *your* extraordinary life.

Question 1

What is your purpose in life? What do you feel you were born to do?

_____
_____
_____
_____
_____
_____
_____
_____

Question 2

What are you doing when you experience your 'Flow State'?

_____
_____
_____
_____
_____
_____
_____
_____

Question 3

Which one of your Chakras do you want to nourish this week?

_____
_____
_____
_____
_____
_____
_____
_____

Question 4

What is your Life Path number? What action step will you take to support your flow?

_____
_____
_____
_____
_____
_____
_____
_____

Question 5

What are your unique, innate gifts and strengths? What value do you add to the world?

_____

_____

_____

_____

_____

_____

_____

_____

Question 6

What small action step can you take to empower your finances this week?

_____

_____

_____

_____

_____

_____

_____

Question 7

What is your highest value? How would you love to fulfil it?

___

Question 8

Which of your four superpowers would you love to master the most right now?

___

Question 9

Which of the 5 life principles could you benefit from today?

_____
_____
_____
_____
_____
_____
_____
_____

Question 10

What is your body type according to Ayurveda? Write your insights below.

_____
_____
_____
_____
_____
_____
_____
_____

Question 11

What simple movement (exercise) would you love to bring into your days? How?

_____
_____
_____
_____
_____
_____
_____
_____

Question 12

How nourishing is your food intake? What can you do to improve it?

_____
_____
_____
_____
_____
_____
_____
_____

Your Reflections

Contact

www.extraordinarylifemagazine.com

Advertising Inquiries + Article Inquiries

Media Opportunities

Production Team

Project Management: Emily Gowor

Editing: Emily Withers

Content Review: Rae Antony & Emily Gowor

Images Source: Shutterstock + Pexels

Typesetting: Chandrashekar Yadav

Disclaimer

The opinions expressed in *Extraordinary Life* are not necessarily those of the publisher(s). Advice is non-specific and does not necessarily substitute medical, psychological, or professional advice for health and wellbeing issues. We do not make any claims that anything published in this magazine is a cure for any disease, ailment, or problem experienced by the reader(s). The magazine is not affiliated with any religious group or religious teaching. *Extraordinary Life* takes no responsibility for the content of advertisements. *Extraordinary Life* may alter the size, content, or position of an article or advertisement where necessary. Articles, adverts, or any other part of this magazine is not to be reproduced without the prior permission of the publisher Gowor International Publishing, and all requests must be made in writing.

www.ingramcontent.com/pod-product-compliance
Ingram Content Group UK Ltd.
Pitfield, Milton Keynes, MK11 3LW, UK
UKHW061212180426
11947UKWH00028B/2005